We are Poets!

2023 Year 5 Kingfishers and Robins' class.

Contents:

Introduction

As part of our writing projects in Year 5 at school we were inspired by the poem 'Magic Box.' We analysed and read the poem together before writing our own class versions of the poem. After this we then all took the time to consider what we would add to our own 'Magic Box' and how it would be made.

Finally, we typed up our creative poems and put them together in our own printed anthology. We really hope that you enjoy it!

Care has been taken to ensure that the work in this book is as authentic as possible, although some spelling and formatting errors have been edited by the teachers the content of your children's poems is still the same. To abide by GDPR regulations all surnames of children have been removed as well as our school's name.

This collection of poems is designed to celebrate and enjoy the creative writing of children in Year 5 this year and has not been published to make profit. Please share this with your families and friends, we will also be keeping a copy in our school library.

The Magic Box, by 5B

We will put in the box

An exquisite sprinkle of kindness and respect,

The glistening rainbow of our languages and cultures,

And the comforting arm of a helpful friend.

We will put in the box

Long twisted vines decorating our Forest School,

The gentle chirping of birds calling you to nature,

And the laughter of innocent children to warm your soul.

We will put in the box

Gentle words of encouragement from our wonderful

teachers,

The bright spark of learning igniting in our brains,

And the rustling of pages as we write inspirational work.

Our box is fashioned from sharp pencils, awards and glue

sticks with lost lids,

With memories, smiles and achievements in the corners,

Its hinges are the strong friendships we form.

We shall surf in our box

On the stardust of our potential where we shimmer,

sparkle and shine

We know that we are well prepared for our futures ahead.

5C The Magic Box

We will put in our box

The earthy scent of pencil sharpenings

Excitement buzzing around like a swarm of bees

And winged books, which soar high above our heads

We will put in our box

Kingfisher feathers orange like the skin of a sour mandarin

The soothing notes of Lofi Girl on repeat

And a wise capybara, who knows all of the answers

We will put in our box

Whiteboard pens that actually work

The joyful laughter of playing children

And a lazy bear, who gives the best hugs

Our box is fashioned from hard work, creativity and team work

With tangled ivy on the lid and sparkle in the corners

We shall learn in our box

About kindness and column multiplication

Then we will dance on our tables

To the sound of the lunchtime bell

Adil's Magic Box
By Adil

I will put in my box
A subzero watermelon iced tea on a Friday afternoon
A glistening golden ballon'dor on a Monday morning
And the soft dough of gulab jamuns on a Tuesday morning

I will put in my box
The sweet scent of luxurious perfume, which fills the air
A crispy bag of mouthwatering ready salted crisps
And the sound of tsunami like waves crashing on boulders

I will put in my box
An ice-cold Pepsi with a squeeze of lime
A hard football, which could bounce to the moon
A yellow moon and a white sun

My box will be made out of hard work, creativity and steel.
With honesty in the corners and iron on the lid.

I will score a goal in my box
Into a goalpost on the pitch-black moon
And I will celebrate by doing a knee slide
into the shimmering stars

Alexandra's Magic Box
By Alexandra

I will put in my box,
The scent of mouthwatering cheese pizza on a Tuesday afternoon,
The sounds of me and Nikoletta laughing every day after school,
And the black and white pandas, that cover my face every night,

I will put in my box,
A sassy panda, who knows everything about bamboo,
The feeling of uncontrollable laughter,
The sound of my mouse clicking onto Roblox

I will put in my box,
The feeling of when my mum buys me Roblox,
The bright colours of my new pens,
The smell of the pages in new books

My box is fashioned from friendship
With our fingerprints in blue, pink, yellow and white
Its hinges are made from glitter

I will play Roblox in my box
Then dance on tables
And throw cake at the crowds

Anas' magic box
By Anas

I will put in my box
The sound of a peeling wrapper from a brand-new Samsung phone,
The smell of a brand-new candle with a fruity tang scent,
And the taste of a soft and sweet doughnuts.

I will put in my box
Fresh Pepsi max straight from the fridge,
The sweet taste of the crunchy outside of jalebi,
And Mouthwatering cheesy margherita pizza, the Italian way.

I will put in my box
A sleepy big capybara,
The sound of a brand-new keyboard,
And the sound of a gigantic brand-new car engine

My box is fashioned from paper and cardboard with paint on the
lid with video game DVDs on the side.
Its hinges are made from professional sketchbooks.

Anna's Magic Box
By (Anna)

I will put in my box
A pencil scratching the paper as I draw,
Steps leading to beautiful vibrant nature,
And a cloud like hamster, who is as quick as a racing car.

I will put in my box
A relaxing melody repeating over and over again,
A fresh Margarita pizza ordered to a decorated table,
And the chirping beautiful birdsong flying from ear to ear

I will put in my box
A snowflake, which is as fast as a snail that drops on my hand,
Chatting with friends,
And a warm blanket that can wrap the whole world.

My box is fashioned from a green glittery box
With vines surrounding it.
On the lid will be imagination and fireworks.
Its hinges are made from wood and kindness.

I shall learn in my box
About how kindness works and art,
Then I will have fun
And it will help me with life.

Brajan's Magic Box
By (Brajan)

I will put in my box

A capybara eating a broken watermelon

Futuristic cars flying over our heads

Mouthwatering rosu on a Sunday afternoon

I will put in my box

A horse driving a Bugatti Chiron

Reaching level 500 in call of duty

My heart pounding when Lewandowski scores a bicycle kick
I will put in my box

The laughter when I make my friends laugh

The happiness when I got my neon scooter

The happiness I get when I race and win

My box is fashioned from happiness it has horses on the lid and its hinges are made of chupacabras nails

Diego's Magic Box
By (Diego)

I will put in my box
A majestic fun fair, where I could laugh
Spending all day with my playful dog
And the smell of cheese burgers, that make you drool

I will put in my box
A red sun and a blue moon covered in cheese
A happy family jumping for joy
And stinky feet that worked hard at school

I will put in my box
Wings that will fly me to Hawaii
With a sketchbook full of creativity
And a room full of happiness

My box is fashioned from titanium
With a lid of steel
And soft cushions in the corners

I will sleep in my box
For ten years
In the King's bed
Until the next coronation

Eknoor's Magic Box
By Eknoor

I will put in my box,
The sweet sound of chicken curry sizzling,
The perfume scent that I could smell forever,
And a Colourful fan which flies across my box,

I will put in my box,
Laughing voices that spread across the school,
Pictures filled with children,
And magical elephants that glisten.

I will put in my box,
Fun Fairs and movies to enjoy,
Kindness that spreads with joy,
And mouth-watering cheesy pizza.

My box is fashioned from friendship
With fireworks and rainbows painted on the lid,
Its hinges are made from glue and covered with nerves,

In my box I will,
Play my favourite game Roblox,
Then eat my mouth-watering pizza.

The Magic Box
By Emma

I will put in my box
Birds chirping on a Sunday morning flying in the air,
My mom's recipe of pasta with extra sauce and toppings on a
Friday evening, And ducks walking in our neighbourhood quacking.

I will put in my box
The luxurious taste of coco ice cream on a Monday,
The feeling of laying in my bed after a long day at school,
And my adorable chick nugget plush I snuggle with all night.

I shall do in my box drawing while in bed while watching the
beautiful landscape of the moon and stars out of my bedroom
window,
Then I will have fun with friends and learning in school.

My box will be fashioned from paper with cute drawings and clouds
And on the sides will be rainbows with panda stickers on the lid.

<u>Isla's Magic Box</u>
By Isla

I will put in my box
Mouthwatering sweets travelling from my throat to my stomach,
The quiet paths in Spain soothing my body and my mind,
And the tasty pizza on a Tuesday at school.

I will put in my box
My precious drawings which I treasure with all my heart,
The calming feeling of my parents' love,
And the intoxicating smell of my rich and special perfume,

I will put in my box,
The satisfying sound of my feet crossing the smooth stones,
My colourful set of pencils, that colour and draw,
And the thrill of travelling inside a giant aeroplane

My box is fashioned from wood and fabric
With rainbows on the lid
And its hinges are made from my imagination.

JAN'S Magic Box
By Jan

I will put in my box
A race track with godly customised Supra's MK4's for me and
friends
A shiny and perfect golden glove
Godlike cats playing with fantastic and adorable capybaras

I will put in my box
Death metal playing on repeat sinking into my ears
Then bright and green sun slightly burned my skin relaxing me
Sights of beautiful Polish rivers helped me calm down

I will put in my box
A dream mansion furnished by masters with shelves filled with
food
A giant football pitch with the one and only all mighty equipment
A replica of the glorious forest school but with 10 times bigger
trees

My box will be furnished with
Climbing walls because I love climbing
The hinges will be made of footballs

I will play football in my box
I will race my friends with cars
And I will relax looking at the polish views and sunbathing

Mayar's Magic Box

By Mayar

I will put in my box

A mouthful of colourful doughnut on a Wednesday

The smell of pepperoni pizza on a Tuesday morning

And delicious eggs in the morning

I will put in my box

A flying unicorn, who is colourful.

A comfortable sofa in front of the tv.

And the feeling of a fluffy cat.

I will put in my box

The sound of Miss Crawford's lovely singing.

And a piano melody, which echoed in my ears

Mikolaj's Magic Box

By Mikolaj

I will put in my box

A scared brown dog,

The glaze of the newest movie

And four plane tickets to Poland.

I will put in my box

The bombardment of colourful fireworks on new year,

A huge 1.1m deep pool in Poland

And the largest game of life board game.

I will put in my box

A mansion with 50 luxurious rooms,

Me beating Roblox doors

And the experience of the epic scenes of Beyblade burst.

My box is fashioned with high tech plates

With hinges made out of Beyblades

And a guarding dog on the lid.

I will live in my box

In a world with no football

Then I will play video games in real life.

Nathan's Magic Box
By Nathan

I will put in my box
A machine that does whatever you want, especially maths.
Delicious mouthwatering gulab jamuns.
And a cottage full of flying, astonishing German shepherds.

I will put in my box
My cultural Nigerian afang soup and garri.
An indoor football house.
And sticky pancakes with maple syrup.

I will put in my box
A radical skating alley.
And dazzling football trophies that can blind any eye in sight.

My box is fashioned from potatoes
With a rainbow on the lid
Its hinges are made from silky soft clouds, as soft as a cat's fur.

Nikola's Magic Box

By Nikola

I will put in my box,

Mouthwatering, sour mandarins

A refreshing cola after my morning run.

And a bee who buzzed in my morning ears

I will put in my box

Pandas and capybaras, who are the kindest animals

Family and friends because they are important

And pierogi, which is my favourite food

I will put in my box

A snowflake on my tongue.

My friends, who are Ola Zuza Niki

And a mouth-watering Mc Flurry from McDonalds

My box is fashioned with shiny stars, diamonds, and metal

And on the lid is stars and squares.

Nikoletta's Magic Box

By Nikoletta

I will put in my box

The echoing sound of Ola and I laughing uncontrollably

The joy of secrets being spread at sleepovers

And the soft bark of my puppy

I will put in my box

The smell of cheese pizza every Tuesday

The chatting of Ola and I walking home

And the feeling of delicate dog fur

I will put in my box

The feeling of a warm breeze shining on me every morning

The sweet smell of fragrant perfume

And the warm feeling of lying in bed before sleep

My box is fashioned from creativity and dreams

With glimmering stars on the lid

Its hinges are made from imagination

With a sprinkle of glitter in every corner

I will laugh in my box

Until salty tears roll down my cheeks

Ollie's magic box

By Ollie

I will put in my box

Majestic magic potatoes,

Thanos's infinity gauntlet

And the colossal milky way

I will put in my box

A dancing parrot and corgi,

the dreaded cheese touch

And a cursed gem from a temple made 9000 years ago

I will put in my box

The smell of melting cheese on a Costco pizza,

The menacing sound of Venus and Saturn combined

And the incredible Champion's League trophies

My box is made of rubies and obsidian

It has emerald corners

Encrusted with mini diamonds

I shall live in my box

On a luxurious cruise ship

Then play in a water park

Salal's Magic Box

By Salal

I will put in my box

A fresh bottle of Pepsi filled to the brim

The tropical scent of skittles on a Saturday

And a fiery red bag of perfectly pointed Doritos

I will put in my box

The pride of a perfectly finished drawing

A bag of mouthwatering gummies from the mosque shop

And the point of a razor-sharp pencil,

Ready to be dragged across a piece of paper

I will put in my box

A flavourful carton of squash

A giant snickers bar from the cupboard

And a bubbly sour can of lemonade

My box is fashioned from balls of crumbled paper

With piles of books on the lid

Its hinges are made from spider webs.

I will swing across giant skyscrapers in my box

And land safe in my bed.

Saloni's Magic Box

By Saloni

I will put in my box

The sweet blossom scent of my new perfume

Small, silly pictures of me when I was younger

And a set of a magical fairy wings

I will put in my box

The sizzling sound of puris being fried in my mom's kitchen

Various magical creatures from all over the world

And the best parts of my favourite songs playing on repeat

I will put in my box

The laughing voices of my friends when I tell them a joke

All of my best art pieces which everyone loves

And the funniest words from my favourite books

My box is fashioned from the most expensive diamonds

With stars on the lid and friendship in the corners.

Its hinges are made from sunshine on a warm summer day

I will play my favourite video game in my box

Then I will play Lego

While eating a yummy bucket of popcorn

Sana's Magic Box

By Sana

I will put in my box

The appetising and mouth-watering Tuesday pizza

100 kittens, parrots and owls staring

The strong scented perfume of my Beloved mom

I will put in my box

5 years of Beaulieu

The sounds of the rainfall that goes infinite

And my teachers, who make my day every time

I will put in my box

Sounds of pandas biting bamboo

Luxurious summer crew

And having a disco every Friday.

My box is made of

Fragile glitter

On the lids is sunsets stickers

And its hinges are made from steel.

I will spend the whole day in my box

Sami's Magic Box

By Seyed

I will put in my box

The mouthwatering pizza that filled me up with joy and satisfaction

Sweaty armpits after a Tuesday morning of intense football battles

I put in my box the bell for lunch that fascinated me with glory

I will put in my box

People shouting with happiness after the teacher added ten minutes to our beloved break

The tsunami of sand and sweat after PE

The intense running in a game of bull dog

I will put in my box

Smiles on people face when they reached a new level of the favourite game

Ronaldo scoring in the last minutes of the world cup final

My box is fashioned from sportsmanship

With footballs on the lid

its hinges are made from Ronaldo's boots

Shivaanch's Magic Box

By Shivaanch

I will put in my magic box

a blue and white bike

A white football

And a magic mountain lion with magic power

I will put in my magic box

A baby lion.

A magic pen that can write everything in the world

And a shiny rainbow apple.

My box will be made out of diamonds.

Sia's Magic Box
By Sia

I will put in my box
The mouthwatering scent of cheesy pizza on a Tuesday lunchtime
The fragrant tulips that spread across the playground
And an adorable kingfisher, who loves to eat oranges,
Like the colour of her feathers

I will put in my box
My friends and teachers' wonderful smiles of happiness
My mom's legendary cooking of delicious food
And a giant scoop of ice cream that me and my friends eat
together

I will put in my box
Thousands of kind hearted bunnies that are dancing
The beautiful sun that shines in the sunlight
And amazing platters with delicious food on them

My box is fashioned from gold and glitter.
With vines and flowers on the lid.
Its hinges are made from plastic.

Sndoos' Magic Box
By (Sndoos)

I will put in my box,
The joy and laughter of Grizzy and the Lemmings
The taste of appetising, fresh, and freezing Zam Zam water
And my best friends and my parents, who are the best in the
world

I will put in my box
The sound of Maghrib adhan, which echoes through the mosque
The luxurious, Kurdish dress that makes you look more glamorous
than ever
And a Unicorn kitty that can soar through the mythical sky

I will put in my box,
The mouthwatering taste of ice coffee from McDonald's
The fluorescent scent of delightful flowers
And a souvenir from Paris, which is the Eiffel tower

My box is fashioned with diamonds, molten rocks, and sweets
The lid is made of mica
And Its hinges are made out of hard work, studying and
creativity

I will do taekwondo in my box
In a trampoline park
Doing really cool things in the air.

Surjot's magic box
By (Surjot)

I will put in my box
A bag full of fun toys and games like Ludo and Fortnite.
I will put a house full of toys that have the coolest things in.
I will have all the happiness for every single day of P.E

I will put in my box
The best pizza from the BT primary school.
I will have a magical pet just for me.
I will have a Pegasus with immortal powers like the magic flight.
I will have a portal of endless stationary that works.
I will have stationary like pens, glues whiteboard pens etc

In my box I will put
Some magical ribbons of the magnificent and beautiful 5C
classroom
I will have in my box a supreme radio
That will have the most relaxing sound on a Friday afternoon.
In my box I will put all the glee of me and my friends Alaa Saloni
Eknoor Sana.

My box will be fashioned from friendship and teamwork
I will have lots of fireworks in the middle
and some glitter on the corners to make it sparkle
Its hinges will be made out of book titles.

Timurs's Magic Box
By Timurs

I will put in my box
Birds singing on Monday morning
Fluffy potatoes melting in my mouth
And the smell of delicious KFC

I will put in my box
My steps in nature
Walking on jagged rocks
And my friends cheering for me playing football

I will put in the box
Yellow sky and a blue sun
A hot beach with sand everywhere
And my mum driving a cool car

My box will be fashioned from hard gold
With Prime in every side
And sharp spikes on the lid
Saving my dreams from other people

Zuzanna's Magic Box
By Zuzanna

I will put in my box
A collection of my precious class photos.
My teacher's smile lit up my heart.
A treasure chest of pierogi.

I will put in my box.
A Tuesday pizza day.
A hug making me smile to my eyes.
A majestic jewel shimmering in my precious eyes.

I will put in my box.
Tsunami of cats floating around me.
A glamorous dress from my family's weddings.
My best friend's koala eyes are looking straight into my soul.

My box is made of comfortable teddies
With shimmering glitter around it
And pictures of Beaulieu.
The hinges will be made of gold
And the love sprinkled around the edges with cat stickers.

Inside my box will be
A disco where we fly to a Polish restaurant while having a slumber
party.

Keayden Magic Box
By Keayden

I will put in my box
A multi coloured shining snake.
Bests pepperoni pizza on a Saturday night.
A wild swim on a best pool at the deep end.

I will put in my box
A gard wizard with a magic wand that glows
A camouflage military custom with a military car
A fabulous sports car that has a v/8 engine that goes 100mph

I will put in my box
A luxurious cloth that is fashioned by Neptune

(Tola) Magic Box
By Omotola

I will put in my box
A drop of orange Lucozade
The smell of Ocra Soup cooking in my dad's kitchen
The squeaking sounds of the Bars and Vault

I will put in the box
The sound of my First Girlfriend by Tytus
The joy of when I win a competition
The sound of a Football and Basket-ball

I will put in my box
The feeling when I score a Hat-trick
The smell of Pounded-Yam
The memories of me and my brother

My box is fashioned from wood and strong metal
With pictures of me and my family on the lid
And its hinges or made from pieces of the Beam.
I will do high Ariels and Back lay-outs in my box
And play football and basketball.

AADAM'S Magic Box
By Aadam

I will put in my magic box

My dark blue, shiny car (from my loving mum)
That makes a scraping sound because
The wheel is wedged up

I love challenging puzzles so
I will put in my box rubix-cube
that I can play with
for hours and still not get bored

I will put in my magic box
My Xbox because I like playing with
my brother -we keep on getting great
things!
The smell of apple juice that I have as a treat
And the sweet taste of juicy raisins

I will put in my magic box
My old iPad that was thrown out the window
It now only plays stick-man

My blue headphones to block out loud noises in school
Good maths games because I like maths

My magic box is fashioned from metal chairs and a lid of nice
memories,
The hinges are made of children's laughter, the
Corners are made of dried glue sticks

Alia's magic box

I will put in the box

Blistering late night shopping and driving,

The mouthwatering smell of amazing pancakes

waiting for me on the breakfast table,

And precious moments with my warm-hearted family.

I will put in my box

The sounds of satisfying jingling pennies,

My meaningful prayers to God

and going to the mosque.

I will put in my box

wonderful memories of celebrating exciting festivals,

The smell of a new book inviting me to new adventures.

And he beautiful orange sunset in Egypt.

My box is fashioned from my best friends on the hinges.

With my family on the sides

And my name on the lid.

I shall surf in my box

Through the wonderful memories I have made in the past.

(Cristina) The Magic Box
By (Cristina)

I will put in the box...
The loud footsteps of me sprinting to bed sneakily even though
my mum hears it.
Receiving tight hugs from my
wonderful mum.

I will put inside the box...
Seeing my younger cousins wanting
to play a game.
Gracefully playing in the garden
when it's sunny and bright.
Smelling the sweet flowers pollinated
by honey bees.

I will put inside the box...
Memories of my cheerful dogs whose
barking flows in my mind.

(Guntaz) Magic Box
By (Guntaz)

I will put in the box
The sweet cuddles from my hard-working mum,
The exquisite feeling of going to town with my dad,
The heartwarming feeling of going to the park with my brother.

I will put in the box
Eating mouthwatering ice cream with my friends,
The blazing hot sun shining on me,
Going on peaceful vacations with my loving family.

I will put in the box
Visiting the glorious Gurdwara with my loving mum,
The beautiful smell of my roses in my garden making me feel alive,
The refreshing breeze embracing my skin.

My box will be made from
A diamond Ruby stone and my parents' engagement ring
It is where all my memories are safe.
I will fly in my box of memories and I will remember them all.

(Hayaat) The magic Box
By (Hayaat)

I will put in the box…
The goodnight kisses my mom gives me
Giggling as I`m playing with my brother,
And the sand going through my toes when I'm at the beach

I will put in the box…
The tight cuddle I give my mom when I see her
And the smile of my brother when he sees me
The heartwarming memories flowing back to my head

I will put in the box
Walking with my family to the park in the summer breeze
The aroma smell of my mum's cooking that I'm impatient to eat
Feeling joy as hugging my brother when I see him when school is
finished

Jasme's Magic Box

By Jasme

I will put in my box,

My brother kissing me goodbye each morning,

My mum hugging me tightly every day,

And my dad waking up early and kissing

Me sneakily when he leaves for work.

I will put in my box

Joyful hugs from my cousins when I surprised them in India,

Memories from me and my family visiting India after 12 years,

And my family meeting together while crying at airport

I will put in my box

My baby toys that I have had since I was born.

My box is fashioned from glass

And diamonds, its hinges are made up of friendship.

Jayden's Magic Box

By Jayden

I will put in my box

A lovely bark from my dog

A kid screaming as he punches a boxing bag

Big hugs from my mum that make me happy

I will put in my box

A lovely smile from Mrs.B,

The song from a peaceful bird tweeting,

And the happy feeling inside you when you feel loved

My box is made of diamonds and emeralds

I shall swim in my box of memories

Hardeep's Magic Box

By Hardeep

I will put in my magic box
Sounds of my siblings laughing,
The smell of mouth-watering pierogi made
By my mum,
And the crashing waves from my first time at the beach

I will put in my magic box
Every minute that I've played with my toys,
The safe soft feeling of my bed when I go to sleep and
The exquisite smell of the fresh summer air.

I will put in my magic box
Sounds of my siblings crashing cars and enjoying their game,
Playing with my cousins,
And the responsibility I felt when I was given my first phone

My box is made from
Glittering gold and diamonds
with shimmering sparkles and fluffy clouds underneath.
Beautiful gold lights that shimmer to music

I will fly in my box high above the skyscrapers
And I will land on the mountain of memories.
After that I will have a good rest.

Jigar's Magic Box

By Jigar

I will put in the box, the lapping waves of a tranquil beach,

The adventurous feeling of a school trip,

And a young baby's innocent smile.

I will put in my box,

The divine feeling of snow melting,

The crying of my little sister that brings me joy,

And the feeling of reading a good book, that transports me to a new world.

I will put in my box,

the majestic feeling of visiting India,

Playing football when it is sunny,

And my phone vibrating telling me that my friends are calling.

My box is made of steel and juicy chicken nuggets,

In my box I will spin and visit India, remembering good Memories.

Noah's Magic Box

By Noah

I will put in the box,

The purple hue from a sun-setting sky,

The picture of me and my brother at the arcade,

And the smell of Japanese knot coffee beans

I will put in the box

A hug from my loving nan

A cuddle from a ginger Welsh cat

And the bowling ball I use at Hollywood bowl which brings me luck

I will put in the box

The comforting smell of the first rain in weeks

The mouthwatering taste of a good chicken curry

And the sound of snow crunching under my feet

My box is fashioned from

Marble and the hinges are made from strong friendships

And stars shall cover the roof

I will swim in my box, from memory to memory

Where I finally stop to bowl and climb

Peter's Magic Box

By Peter Syvovol

I will put in my box

Going on a walk with my loving parents
Playing exciting computer games

And listening my favourite songs.

I will put in my box

Watching the lovely YouTube

Going on a late shopping trips

And eating delicious sweets in the evenings

I will put in my box

Talking with friends

Going to a swimming pool

And going on a super long trip.

Miya's Magic Box

By Miya Tanner

I will put in my box

The glint of my head band shining in the sun,

The noise of my notification as a friend messages me,

and the laugh of Sarina telling me a funny joke

I will put in my box

The way that my mouth waters as I open a delicious bar of chocolate,

My cheeky smile that you can see from a mile away,

And warm snuggles from my cat

That lays on my lap as we watch TV

Amayah`s Magic Box

By Amayah Taylor

Carefully, I will add to my magic box

The glint in my eye as I talk with my friends

And the alarming noise of a notification on my phone

I'll add to my box

The comforting arm of my best friends

And us glimmering in the beautiful sun

I will add to my box

Peaceful thoughts of my daily diary

And my morning and night skincare routine

Ramadan's Magic Box

By Amadou

I will put in my box

The calm sound of Quran Recitation

I will put in my box

The feeling of a football under my feet

The strong vibrations of my controller as I play FIFA 23

A boost of friendship and a hug from family.

A vibrant sound of a phone notification from a friend.

I will put in my box

The exquisite sight of the Dubai Sunset at the beach

The satisfying feeling of sand gripping onto my toes.

My box is made out of tight unbreakable friendship

I will swim through the memories of my older life

and feel excited for my future.

Roxely's Magic Box

By Roxely

I will put in my box

Deep footprints in the first snowfall

The fresh smell of the first rainfall

And the orange sunset that glows in the sky

I will put in my box

A sprinkle of laughter that lights my heart

Family memories from when I was younger

And the laughs of my little siblings

I will put in my box

The warm cuddles from my mum,

The delicate aroma of spices that runs through the house

And caring smiles from my family

My box will be made from

Memories and pictures

and its hinges will be made of strong friendship without

judgement

I will walk through the world with my box

To share happiness and

Memories whilst adding to it every day.

Sarco's box

I will put inside the box me and my family playing games together.

My dad's trip to his home country of Iraq for his birthday.

The loving sound of my family laughing.

I will put inside the box

Listening to my baby cousin cry

Seeing my family go their home country

And my friend's laughing, which always makes me smile.

My box is made from a sea of emotions.

I will swim through memories of me and my family

going out in the middle of the night for fun.

Sarina's Magic Box

I will put in my box

The warm hugs that I get from Zahra,

The tearing sound of birthday wrapping paper,

And the touch of a pillow when having a pillow fight

with my brother

I will put in my box

The fresh smell of delicious pizza,

The light from the sun shining outside,

And the smell of delight from vanilla house incense,

I will put in my box

My loud laughter as Miya tells me a funny joke,

The rustling sound from leaves dancing on branches,

The kind smiles from friends and family which makes me feel happy

My box is made from

Gold that glistens with the brightness of a sunset,

On the lid will be all my memories,

The hinges are made from steel,

And in the corners are stickers that shine in the light,

I shall draw in my box

And display it on a marble wall in a fascinating art gallery.

Wardah's Magic Box

By Wardah

I will put in my box

The first snowfall of winter

The smell of the salty waves

And a tight cuddle from my mum

I will put in my box

Late night shopping with my mum, where we buy shoes and clothes

The smell of the first rainfall after a long, dry summer day

and the orange sunset melting into the sky.

I will put in my box

The delicate aroma of spices that runs through the house

My box is made from memories and happiness

I will walk as far I can to share my happiness with everyone.

Zahra's Magic Box

By Zahra

I will put in my box

The peaceful enjoyment with my family,

My adorable baby sister playing with me,

A bubbling fried egg and delicious dal cooked lovingly by my mum,

I will put in my box

My BFF Sarina because she cares for me,

The tweeting birds that come around when I say hi to Sarina's mum,

I like it when my friends introduce me to their game and discover new games
with my   friends.

I will put in my box

Maths in school where I feel like a real pro,

My favourite teacher giving me cuddles and her name is Mrs Bullingham,

Entering forest school because it is like I am connecting with nature.

My box is made of fluff, and on the lid, it has a picture of my most special
friends. The hinges are made out of metal and in the corners are hearts.

I will swim in my box of memories,

I will make it at my house,

It is like my life my life has refreshed,

And I will add more memories each day.

Patrik's Magic Box

By Patrik

I will put in my box

a fast blue and yellow bike

and a strong supercar

I will put in my box

my amazing friends

and the smell of the cold air on Christmas morning

I will put in my box my super school

My box is fashioned from gold with rocks on the lid and trees in the corners.

Its hinges are made from branches

I will surf in my box then save it in a special place

Vici's Magic Box

I will put in my box a grey and black cat
I will put in the box a green and white football

I want to put my mum in my box because she gives the warmest
hugs.

(Valko) Magic Box

By Valko Ivanov

I will put it the box

The smile of loved ones warming my heart

Birds singing songs and flying way up in the sky

Looking at the ticking clock waiting for it to be home time

I will put in my box

Playing my favourite game when I get home

And nature's vines wrapping around trees like there's zero gravity

I will put in my box

Getting happy when I finish a drawing

I will put in my box

Memorable days with my friends

And a big bubble of love that won't pop

My box is made out of pure meteorite

And diamonds made from Saturn's ring

And I will put it in a top tier safe

Tyler's Magic Box

I will put in the box,

A bright red and blue microphone that converts singing into a game,

My incredible singing,

And my brother's high-pitched singing voice

I will put in the box,

The warm sound of my nan's parrot and my mischievous cats,

Games with memorable voices that I am now used to by now

And my church Leader's exquisite voice

I will put in the box,

A soft and gentle kiss before I lay in my comfy bed

The sound of a delicate lullaby hugging me to sleep,

And the warming sound of family laughter.

My box is fashioned with,

Shining 24 carat gold,

Sparkles of all the good times we had throughout the years,

And a wonderful feeling of happiness.

I will surf in my box,

Through the seas of memories of my life,

And over wild waves of everything I enjoy.

Sean's magic box

I will put it in my box...

The smell of the delicious food that refreshes your mind.

Clinking coins crashing into each other in my pocket.

I will put it in my box...

The colourful blooms of my achievements,

Innocent smiles of a baby,

a pink glistening sunset that glows in your soul

And nights when I snuggle up with my family watching a movie

I will put in my box...

The delicate aroma of the flowers roaming around my house

The embrace of a gentle breeze,

The flow of the river

And a sea of memories covering souls like petals falling

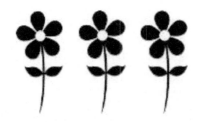

Springing Forward -5B

Curious creatures wake up to a different world

A world full of longer, lighter days

Stretching from their beds, where they have been curled

Beginning to bathe under the sun's warming rays

This marks the end of harsh, cold winters

Rainbow bulbs begin to bud and bloom

Blanketing the ground in a sea of glimmering flowers

Their delicate scents cover the previous gloom

Inviting you to rest in their peaceful meadows for hours

Buzzing worker bees pass the message that spring has sprung

Air fills with the welcome laughter of children playing outside

As sunlight peeks from behind thick cotton clouds

That part to allow it to shine again on the world

Warmth from the sun welcomes new life to earth

As curious animals take their first, bumbling steps

Dirt hides under fingernails whilst we plant new seeds to awaken

Dreams of rainbow vegetables that will be ready for peaceful
summer picnics

The hopes of many cloudless days, with visits to the beach

and brighter nights that melt into beautiful sunsets

Every season has its own magic, and spring brings the promise of summer.

Spring Poem 5C

Spring is here, the world is yawning

Waking from her deep Winter sleep

Glorious birdsong signifies morning

As the sunrise smiles over fields of sheep

Enchanting blossom adorns trees like jewels

An intoxicating sight after winter so cruel

Daffoldils stand proudly saluting the sun

A carpet of bluebells shout Spring has begun

Lawnmowers hum just after dawn

And farmers prepare to sow their corn

Easter brings forth children's delight

As brave hungry chicks take their first flight

The Summer season beckoned ever nearer

Those baking hot days are just within sight

The circle of life becomes much clearer

With the crystal clarity of evenings so bright